MW01172218

BECOMING AUTHENTICALLY AFRICAN

A GUIDE TO EMBRACING CULTURE IN EVERYDAY LIFE

ZOE SARABO

Becoming Authentically African
A Guide to Embracing Culture in Everyday Life
Copyright © 2024 by Zoe Sarabo

Printed in the United States of America

Author: Zoe Sarabo

Expert Contributor: Oloye Oladipupo Olanrewaju, Borokini Awo of Odewale Land (pg. 102)

ISBN: 979-8-9918727-1-3 (Paperback)
Library of Congress Control Number: 2024924528

Editor & Book Cover Design: Jvion Jones

Published by: Ahvision Publishing
Tempe, AZ 85282

www.ahvisionpublishing.com

TABLE OF CONTENTS

TABLE OF CONTENTS

TABLE OF CONTENTS

Authors Note:

I hope this book helps those among us who are unsure of how to start their journey of reconnecting to a heritage that is our birthright.

INTRODUCTION

Based on the education most people have received, the modern African story starts with the occupation of the African continent by European invaders, who used religion and trade as vehicles to conquer and colonize the people of the continent. This process of colonization did not happen overnight. It was a gradual process, beginning in the 1400s with the advent of European technological advancement. Their ability to cross oceans with large numbers of people and products, combined with weaponry that was more advanced, enabled European travelers to reach the soils of the continent to form settlements, establish trade agreements, and impose a new religious doctrine on the natives.

The gun and the Bible became influential tools to conquer the hearts and minds of the inhabitants, along with forming alliances with warring tribes. There is documentation to show trade and imposition of religion as the initial instruments used to win hearts with gifts unfamiliar to the population and minds with a new religion that shifted respect and adulation of African traditional practices to that of the "European God." The infusion of Christianity was not just a shift in the worship of a different God, but it slowly changed elements of African culture that had formed the binding fabric of those societies since the beginning of time.

As the continent was being occupied by foreign invaders, millions of its African population were kidnapped, sold, and shipped to new lands across the oceans to endure over two centuries of enslavement and colonization. The colonization of the African continent, the enslavement of its people in foreign lands, and continued colonization after the end of physical bondage resulted in the theft of resources and exploitation of free labor, thus cementing European global hegemony. The impact of this global African Holocaust was and continues to be significant. Although there are nuances in enslavement and colonization depending on the Nationality of the colonizer, the result remains the same—a significant loss in memory of cultural traditions and practices and shaming of anything African.

To maintain a people in a constant state of mental and physical bondage, there needs to be a system in place to ensure that consideration of an alternative is impossible. Europeans employed several methods to ensure the security of their position of hegemony for centuries:

- Violence that instilled fear
- Religion that taught submission and shame in the African culture

- A subconscious inferiority belief system that elevates whiteness and its cultural value system

Over time, and through consistent retaliation in various ways, Africans on the Continent and in the diaspora were successful in their fight against physical bondage and have made significant gains in reaffirming our humanity and equal rights. However, the struggle to reverse centuries of physical, mental, and spiritual oppression continues today. This book is meant to give direction on steps we should take towards unification and reclaiming our cultural heritage as a collective Pan-African family with the complete understanding that African cultural identity will never return to pre-colonization.

This book is for those of us who have generational lineage in the Western hemisphere, have lost direct connection to our Ancestral heritage, and are seeking ways to 1) reaffirm our African identity and 2) reconnect to the motherland and its people. I firmly believe we are on the cusp of an African Renaissance that is more than a fad or a phase, and with intentional actions, this can lead to a significant shift in the progression and elevation of the African man, woman, family, nation, and culture.

CHAPTER 1
Ideologies That Empower & Elevate

Funtumfrafu Denkyemfrafu
(Unity in diversity)

CHAPTER 1

Ideologies That Empower & Elevate

According to Kwame Ture, "Pan-Africanism is the total Liberation and Unification of the African continent under a socialist system." While I agree with this definition, I would expand by adding Pan-Africanism as the Liberation of the African continent through the unification of the continent with its Diaspora based on economic collaboration and cultural renaissance under a socialist system. If I may be bold, I would posit that the following points should be widely acknowledged as the primary tenets of Pan-Africanism as they express the ideals the term is meant to accomplish.

- Unification of the African continent

- Unification of Africans of the Diaspora and Continental Africans

- A mass cultural movement that places Africa and its Culture at the center

- The intentional act of supporting the growth and elevation of the African Global community through economic support, investment in, and partnering with locals

UNDERSTANDING PAN-AFRICANISM

It is important for me to start with the Pan-African movement because it embodies the principle of continental and Diasporan Africans working together. I believe this is arguably the only way to true self-actualization and freedom for African nations and their people. Therefore, a discussion about the African Diaspora, reconnecting with our cultural heritage, and remembering who we are at our core cannot be done without the spirit of Pan-Africanism at the center.

The Pan African movement began with the organization of political activists and intellectuals from the West Indies, United States, Europe, and Africa between 1900 and 1945. They met six different times to discuss colonial control of Africa and develop strategies for eventual African political liberation (Adejumobi).

The movement can be considered as being the brainchild of Sir Henry Sylvester Williams, "a West Indian Barrister who formed the African Association in London, England, to encourage Pan-African unity, especially throughout the British colonies" (Friends of the African Union, n.d.). He initiated the concept of creating a forum where Africans and African Diasporans could discuss and push a common agenda that sought the unification and freedom of African peoples globally. This forum led to the first Pan African Congress in 1900, which saw the gathering of 37 delegates and 10 other participants and observers in London, England.

"The chair was taken by Bishop Alexander Walters, a leader of the African Methodist Episcopal Zion Church in the United States and president of the National Afro-American Council. The vice chairmen were representatives of independent African states: Frederick Johnson, former Attorney-General of Liberia, and the Haitian Benito Sylvain, aide-de-camp to the Ethiopian emperor" (Kendake).

Understanding the significant role Sir Sylvester Williams played in forming the initial African and African Diaspora groups that became the foundation of Pan-Africanism is key to understanding the history. His role inspired great leaders such as WEB DuBois, who became known as the father of Pan-Africanism. A title that is up for debate, however, credit is due to DuBois for the organization of subsequent Pan African conferences, which were called Congresses:

1st PAC – London, UK 1897

2nd PAC – London, UK 1900

3rd PAC – Paris, France 1919

4th PAC – London, UK 1921

5th PAC – Manchester, UK 1974

Pan-Africanism lives on

There is a lot of information on the early years of the Pan-African movement, including there being three successful and well-attended Congresses held on the continent. These Congresses were:

6th PAC – Tanzania 1974

7th PAC – Uganda 1994

8th PAC (1) – Ghana 2016

The 6th Pan African Congress held in 1974 saw the attendance of two hundred leaders, activists, and organizers arrive in Tanzania. The Congress was hosted by Pan-Africanist and then Tanzanian president Julius Nyerere. It was the first to be held on the continent. Still, he received tremendous support and organizing ideas from Washington D.C. activists, especially SNCC (Student Non-Violent Coordinating Committee) veterans exploring Pan-African work in the area. "Other activists in the larger Black Power Movement, along with Africans associated with liberation movements like South African poet Keorapetse Kgositsile, were instrumental in its success. Greatly influencing all of this was scholar and activist C.L.R. James, who had helped organize the fifth meeting. African and Caribbean embassies made for important network building in the nation's capital" (SNCCdigital).

I was very fortunate to have the opportunity to attend the 8th Pan African Congress hosted by the Ghanaian government in 2016. It was my first time on the continent and being in the presence of activists, intellectuals, politicians, artists, and business owners from across the Continent and Diaspora representing their regions and united with the goal of coming to a consensus on the theme "The Africa We Want."

The question to be asked is, what strategies should we put in place to propel the work of Pan-Africanism? We have a number of individuals today who are stalwarts of the movement and help to keep the fire of the movement lit. What is needed is to go beyond conversations and meetings and to organize strategically with the intention of actively working together to bring to realization the wishes of our Pan-African predecessors.

Here is a list of Pan-African intellectuals I recommend who help shape our understanding of the movement and its status. Each of whom has an organization, group, or institution that is actively involved in the work of Pan-Africanism or is being developed.

- Dr. Umar Ifatunde (also known as Dr. Umar Johnson)
- PLO Lumumba
- Dr. Arikana Chihombori-Quao

- Julius Malema (considered one of the leading voices)
- Maulana Karenga

For those of us who are new to the movement and would like to learn more about its history and leading voices, I would suggest listening to the speeches of:

- WEB Dubois
- Marcus Garvey
- Maulana Karenga
- Julius Nyerere
- Kwame Nkrumah
- Kwame Ture (formerly known as Stokely Carmichael)

What does being a Pan-Africanist mean at an individual level? It means understanding and showing concern for the conditions of Africans on the continent and across the diaspora. It means Participating in activities that support the economic and social expansion of our communities and doing so with the understanding that we are "African first and everything else second" (Dr. John Henrik Clarke).

This book dives deep into action steps that anyone who identifies as African can take to strengthen ties with their cultural heritage and be a part of the Pan-African Movement.

ADOPTING THE PRINCIPLES OF UBUNTU

"Pan-Africanism is vital to our success as African people because, according to Dr. Kofi Osei-Kusi, "Pan-Africanism is UBUNTU. It is a necessary philosophy that should guide and direct us as a collective. It also is the best response to the way the actions of others have impacted how we see ourselves, each other, and the way we love and build together" (TheeAlfaHouse). Ubuntu is a South African Xhosa word meaning "I am because you are. You are because we are."

All societies have principles that serve as a guide to how a group of people should conduct themselves and interact with each other. These principles form the basis of a value and belief system often supported by religious, spiritual, and/or traditional teachings. In establishing a community rooted in an African-centered lifestyle, it would be expected and necessary to have a value system that reinforces who we are as a people and helps move us forward. One such value system is UBUNTU, represented by the proverb "umuntu, ngumuntu, ngabantu," meaning "a person is a person through other people."

For me, it is a reminder that we are all connected, and my presence and achievements would not be possible on my own without the intentional and unintentional love, support, and nurturing of the community. UBUNTU is a necessary guide, particularly during times such as this, when there seems to be a growing division among various segments of the community.

There is no doubt that slavery and colonization have affected the way African peoples interact with each other globally. Additionally, there has been the continued occurrence of neo-colonialism and institutionalized racism that places a further burden on our ability to properly heal and co-exist effectively. We see fractures between Black Men and Women and between Continental Africans and Diaspora Africans that, in varying degrees, have always existed but appear to be widening. Changes in societal expectations, social norms, and the intentional spread of misinformation are some of the factors contributing to the divisions.

I recognize how strong and resilient our people are, having survived and thrived in the shadows of a centuries-long holocaust, followed by periods of colonization, segregation, and apartheid regime. While the above-mentioned oppressive systems no longer exist in their original construct, institutionalized racism and neo-colonization have been ingratiated into the fabric of our societies, influencing how we interact with each other and the direction of our communities.

The effects affect the way we seem to be openly expressive in our frustrations with each other and have contributed to a perceived loss of love and respect for each other. The conversations that are happening publicly on social media tell me that we have chosen to blame each other for our hardships and misguided behaviors rather than recognizing that we are a product of a system that intends to ensure that we are completely under its control. In the face of these difficulties, we continue to succeed, thrive, and show up for each other. However, there is still much work to be done, and our ability to truly overcome cannot happen without the intentional practice of UBUNTU.

In the book EVERYDAY UBUNTU by Mungi Ngomane, we are given several principles that we can adopt in our quest to live with each other the African way. The three principles I found to be useful to adopt are:

1. See Yourself in Other People: People of African descent are the most diverse group of people as a result of the extension of our displacement. Even within the same region and country, we develop varying outlooks on life. However, for Pan-Africanism to be successful, we have to remember that our roots are in Africa, and we share a similar cultural identity beyond slavery and colonization. Therefore, we need to highlight our similarities, which are many, and go beyond the minor differences in the quest for advancement to be successful.

I enjoy listening to African Americans who have taken trips to countries with a large African presence and can experience the local culture. It is pleasing to observe the shift in mindset and the expansion of their perspective when they return from their excursions. They are able to connect and see other Diasporan Africans as brothers and sisters who happen to live in another country.

2. Make Unity A Priority: There have been moments when we have been able to organize among ourselves to speak out against various forms of oppression. However, these organized movements tend to be short-lived and fail to make a lasting impact as needed. With intentional action toward Pan-Africanism and embodying an African-centered lifestyle, it would be easier for us to Unite under common goals and ideals.

I can tell that there is a change in attitude towards Africa and African culture by the Diaspora, whereby there is a growing desire to connect more to our cultural identity and the home of our ancestors. Thanks to the growing popularity of Afrobeats, the success of Black Panther and The Woman King, and the increasing number of Diasporans traveling to the continent, we have made great strides in learning and understanding each other better. I believe that we are taking the right steps towards establishing deeper ties.

3. Choose to See the Wider Perspective: There have been several instances where I've found myself in debates about the perceived distrust between African Americans and Continental-born Africans. There was a particular conversation where an African American friend was upset by the political decision the Ethiopian community made in pulling their support from the Democratic Party in support of a Republican Senate Candidate. The individual shared a video of a group of African Americans accusing Ethiopians of intentionally attempting to work against the interest of the Black community.

I had to explain that there was a violent conflict happening in Ethiopia, and the community felt that switching their support was the best way they were able to gain the attention of politicians and get the respect as a community to be taken seriously. Sometimes, we tend to get caught up in our beliefs that may not be a true reflection of reality, which prevents us from connecting with our family. Having conversations with communities that are not ours and building relationships will help us see the wider perspective.

CHAPTER 2
Recognizing & Overcoming Barriers

Wawa Aba
(Perseverance, toughness)

CHAPTER 2
Recognizing & Overcoming Barriers

The experiences of people of African descent globally have had varying effects depending on the unique construct of individual societies. What has been consistent across all colonies is the restrictions placed on the connection to cultural identity and the presence of a system that maintained the status quo of continued marginalization. However, we were able to reinvent ourselves to better adapt to our new condition, thus creating new cultural identities that included adopting elements of a culture that was alien to our own.

The assimilation into a European culture that is foreign to the African ethos was an inevitable process that resulted in too many of us only seeing ourselves through Eurocentric Ethos. Our worldview and perception of our identity create confusion when confronted with elements of African culture, and we are then forced to question our cultural affiliation. In deconstructing the condition of our double consciousness—a term first coined by W.E.B. Du Bois and later explored by Frantz Fanon—I have identified two conditions that, in my opinion, afflict many in the Diaspora.

First, Imposter Syndrome, and second, the fear of being accused of cultural appropriation. Based on conversations with customers, relatives, and friends about these two conditions, I believe that, like any uncomfortable change we experience, there needs to be a shift in mindset and a process of unlearning. Too many of us with recent enslaved ancestors are having difficulties embracing our African selves. Fortunately, there is a shift happening, and many are gravitating to their African identity and seeking that connection.

IMPOSTER SYNDROME

Over my years in the fashion industry, promoting and marketing African Fashion, I have come to realize that many people have barriers to embracing African Fashion or the lifestyle due to " Imposter Syndrome."

What is Imposter Syndrome?
Imposter Syndrome is a common feeling among many of us. It's when we believe we're not as capable as others think, and we fear that it is only a matter of time before we are exposed as a fraud.

Symptoms
- Self-Doubt
- Feelings of Inadequacy
- Anxiety
- Lack of Self Confidence
- Constant Comparison to other people
- Afraid of being labeled as a fraud

For the purposes of the topic of culture and adopting an African-centered lifestyle, I would define Imposter Syndrome as a condition through which someone does not feel qualified to be associated with African culture. They may fear being seen as a fraud for assuming the lifestyle associated with the culture in a way that does not come naturally to them. Due to unfamiliarity with a specific culture, any attempts to adapt or embrace it may feel uncomfortable and unnatural. Therefore, a decision is made to avoid any association.

This mindset or symptom is as a result of:

- Being stripped of African culture due to slavery, colonization, and sustained exposure to a foreign culture.
- The prevalence of negative images of Blacks and Africans in popular culture, media, cartoons, and documentaries.
- Rhetoric from a segment of a Black community where there is a denial of being African or coming from the African continent.
- Imposter Syndrome reveals itself through comments like "That style is more your thing, not mine," "You have the look for that kind of fashion statement," and "Being natural is not my style. I look better with wigs, and they are easier to manage."

The process of integration and westernization not only means that we lose the African cultural mindset but assimilate a mindset of a dominant culture that is opposite to who we should be at our core. Therefore, because of how an individual was raised and the limited exposure they had to African culture, sudden exposure to an activity, event, or fashion that is Africentric results in conflicted feelings or other feelings of discomfort. Such a person believes they are intruding into or taking on elements of an unfamiliar culture.

The purpose of this book is not only to show ways to adapt and embrace the lifestyle but also to help those with feelings of Imposter Syndrome feel comfortable acknowledging their cultural heritage and knowing that it's their birthright. This concern of being fake or an imposter assumes that there is a certain point in time where ties to the continent are irrevocably severed due to separation. Therefore, it is believed that those of us whose ancestors were enslaved can no longer be considered Africans and deserving of the right to embrace everything that comes with being African.

Although many of us have lost conscious awareness and knowledge of cultural practices, I believe that who we are at our core remains within the essence of our DNA, waiting for the right environment and exposure to express itself. It is all that makes us different from other cultures: the hair texture, the melanin, the unique physical features, and the way we move rhythmically as we create with ease. The way the spirit continues to guide and protect us in the face of adversity is the way we are strengthened (empowered) despite all odds that make us one.

WHAT IS CULTURE?

According to Britannica, culture includes language, ideas, beliefs, customs, codes, institutions, tools, techniques, works of art, rituals, and ceremonies, among other elements. It is the way of life of a society and community.

For the purposes of this book, we will explore the meaning of African and Diasporan Black Culture. Black American culture is a subculture of American culture. It is the way of speech, style of dress, artistic creation, particular ceremonies and rituals, and institutions that are unique to and created by people of African descent born in the United States. Even within the Black community, there are subcultures, depending on Socioeconomic background, region of birth, and the influence of the Black immigrant community.

It is important to note that Culture is fluid and varies depending on changing dynamics within a society. Culture may go through an evolutionary process of creation and expansion, and in many instances, parts of it are lost. For example, within the

Black community, artistic talent has created variations of Black culture over time in response to social conditions created by external factors that have impacted the community in various ways. This is important to note as, like the Afro-Caribbean and Afro-Latino cultures, elements of who we are in response to a system and society that, in their essence, exist to keep the African man and woman demoralized and constricted in a way that maintains their subjugation. Therefore, consciously and unconsciously, we are surviving, living, and creating in response to and despite being under the constant influence of an oppressive system.

Elements of our cultures are fragments of what was passed on over the centuries from Africa. Much of it, as beautiful as it is, also serves as a reminder of our status of once being in bondage. We have several examples of cultural movements across the African diaspora that were formed in response to social and political conditions.

These examples include The Harlem Renaissance (a cultural movement of art, poetry, and storytelling), Hip Hop (started as a voice for the voiceless), Blues, Rastafarianism, Reggae, and Bomba, among others. Each genre continues to have its own energy and message that has allowed it to be impactful globally.

QUESTIONS TO PONDER...

- What do we currently view as Black American culture?
- What influence do our modern artists, singers, and poets have on the larger community?
- Can we identify the modern culture that is being marketed and pushed by Black entertainers and influencers as an accurate representation of Blackness?
- How does the content of Black American culture shape our mindset and how we relate to and interact with each other?

These questions are important because the quality of existence for diasporans comes as a result of being "forced to function within a culture that is based on a worldview that is oppressive to their ethos" (Ani, 4).

It is important to note that culture is the foundation of every successful civilization and should not be underestimated. The argument can be made that culture is America's biggest export because of how the music industry and Hollywood shape the way the rest of the world views the country and its people. This influence has inspired a surge in migration to the United States and led to the popularity of African American music and dance styles around the world.

In studying the rich culture created by African Americans over the years, I am increasingly concerned about the quality of the art being promoted and marketed today. One must ask what values are being espoused, what the message is, and what the general theme and spirit are behind the content.

Currently, the culture being pushed by the music and entertainment industries is mainly one of individualism, materialism, and over-sexualization of the woman's body as a means of acquiring material wealth and access. We no longer have messaging that is positive and uplifting in a way that elevates the community, which is potentially dangerous and destructive to the future of who we are as a people.

Understandably, due to the position of African Americans in society, it was not possible to attain the level of global success it has without the support of White agents who benefit from capitalizing on the community's creativity. However, with the involvement of the same outside groups influencing the creation, packaging, and distribution of content created, Black artists are denied the ability to take control of their artistic creation. There is a system that denies Black artists and the larger community the ability to truly gate-keep the culture. But should there be "gatekeeping," and what would that look like?

What moral values and standards should we subscribe to in order to ensure the healthy functioning of our communities? Within the Black community, there are subcultures based on socioeconomic background, regional differences, and religious background. These factors are fluid, and an individual can change and adapt to a different subculture due to changes in life circumstances and environment.

It is time for an intentional decision about the foundation of Black culture, a clear and unifying set of value systems that guide the collective irrespective of any subculture. This will prevent confusion about what new fad should be considered acceptable and give clear direction to the young generation. The aim should be a culture that reaffirms who we are as African people and engenders a spirit of love, compassion, and brotherhood/sisterhood grounded in cultural knowledge. This is important because the community has, to a large extent, lost control of the art that is created, packaged, and marketed as Black culture.

Unfortunately, much of what is currently being created has destructive content rather than content that uplifts, empowers, inspires greatness, and promotes unity of purpose. We seem to be collectively oblivious to the silent and growing force that is quickly erasing the remaining cultural values. This erasure is easy to occur because, collectively, we lack true knowledge of self and have lost much of our African grounding. Grounding in African-centered morals and values informs the way we interact with each other, the quality of artistic work we produce, and our relationship with nature. Unfortunately, due to the stripping of our identity and our continued exposure and interaction with a culture that is foreign to us, we are becoming a people susceptible to a culture that our ancestors would not recognize.

Despite the direction Black popular culture is going, there are scholars, authors, and artists who are creating content that reminds us of the true essence of who we are. We certainly cannot forget our Spiritual workers, who are doing the work of healing, teaching, and guiding those of us who are seeking guidance and a deeper connection to self.

CULTURAL APPROPRIATION

What is cultural appropriation? According to the Oxford Dictionary, Cultural Appropriation is the unacknowledged or inappropriate adoption of the customs, practices, and ideas of one person or society by members of another and typically more dominant people or society.

As African fashion beyond the dashiki started to become popular, the question of cultural appropriation by communities whose ancestors were enslaved became a topic of discussion among both recently arrived Africans and Diasporan Africans. Also, many were concerned about adorning themselves with fashion pieces that could be seen as an insult to members of a particular Ethnic group associated with the fashion piece. While this can be avoided with education, this concern of possible offense is valid.

Understandably, these concerns as to whether Black communities from the Diaspora can be accused of culturally appropriating the style and fashion derived from Africa were raised by both descendants of those who were once slaves and recent immigrants from Africa. In answering this question, we must first clarify a few points.

A. Can we agree that groups in the diaspora whose fore-parents were enslaved are recognized as having ancestral and cultural lineage to Africa?

B. If yes, can there be a particular date in history after which descendants of the homeland are no longer considered legitimate children of that soil? At what point can that cord of connection be cut?

C. Therefore, If never, can a people with a direct connection to a place appropriate elements of that place?

If we can conclude that diasporan groups who are descendants of enslaved people are still tied to the continent, then the fear of and conversation around cultural appropriation are respectfully misplaced and moot. We should and do have the right to claim ownership of the land and culture and feel comfortable embracing every aspect of being African and lending our skills and resources to the betterment of the continent.

> *"I am not African because I was born in Africa but because Africa was born in me."*
> **Kwame Nkrumah**

However, it must be emphasized that there are practices and customs unique to specific ethnic groups that are considered to be sacred and used for specific cultural rituals or kept for Royalty and, therefore, are meant for special occasions. These practices and customs should be respected and only used with permission by members of the relevant group and within the correct cultural setting. If a fabric, jewelry, or a full outfit is worn outside of the correct cultural setting and without a true understanding of its meaning and significance, then any wearer, whether they are of African descent or not, would be considered as culturally appropriating.

Having been born and raised in Western society for many years makes understanding the social norms second nature. However, due to the complexity of African societies, it will take intentional learning and exposure to understand the norms and practices of various cultures.

For example, it took me many years and multiple conversations with friends before I felt comfortable wearing the Kente print. I understand the history and importance of Kente fabric to the Ghanaian culture. It is a handwoven textile that originates from the Ashanti region in Ghana and was worn exclusively by Kings and their courts. Along with originally representing status and authority, the colors and patterns have distinct names and meanings. Its use gradually expanded from being clothing strictly for royalty to being worn by the larger community for special cultural occasions such as weddings and naming ceremonies. Due to my awareness of its importance to the Ghanaian culture and my love for textiles, I resolved to wear only printed textiles that are made in a factory as opposed to an authentic textile that is handwoven.

On the flip side, our affinity for and ability to comfortably wear Western-style clothing came as a result of centuries of association with Western culture. Over the years, the men's suit and tie and many ladies' styles were adopted by Africans, who had their own form of coverage prior to the arrival of the Europeans. In many cases, the adoption of the Western style of clothing came dipped in shame of the way many African cultures traditionally covered their bodies.

This is to say that we have both learning and unlearning to do with respect to what clothing we choose to wear and how we choose to wear it. The unlearning is understanding that our choice of dress was forced upon us, which coincided with the loss of knowledge of the cultural meanings behind the way we took care of and braided our hair, the meanings of symbols used in our clothing, and the importance of jewelry and other accessories that accompany a style of dress.

We must acknowledge and understand that centuries of indoctrination will not reverse itself without intentional efforts on our part to do the work needed to regain self-understanding. This comes with approaching our traditional practices with humility and a desire to relearn.

CHAPTER 3
Finding Africa In
African-American Culture

Sankofa
(Learning from the past)

CHAPTER 3
Finding Africa in African American Culture

There is no argument that there was an African presence in the Americas prior to the arrival of Christopher Columbus. In fact, there are several books written by explorers, anthropologists, historians, and geologists, both Black and White, who have confirmed that waves of Africans left the continent and settled across the globe. While we acknowledge this fact, it is also true that millions of Africans were brought to the United States to work as slave labor from various parts of primarily West and Central Africa.

Originating from several cultures across these regions, Africans brought with them a rich array of artistic talents and visual expressions that portrayed the skills gained from working in the traditions of their culture. For example, the Edo artists are known for their talents in creating tools and sculptures from Bronze. However, through forced stripping of cultural practices and mixing with European aesthetics, the artistic style of the African American has evolved into a blend of Africa, African Diaspora, and Eurocentric aesthetic values.

Early African American music traditions have their origins in the early African experience of enslavement, which gave birth to slave songs, spirituals, and gospel music. These musical forms were the syncretization of "African chanting practices and song styles" with "worshiping styles" that were Christian in nature (Brooks 957). Slave Songs served the purpose of delivering hidden messages to enslaved Africans seeking comfort in difficult moments or assistance in their quest to escape. Spirituals and Gospels evolved out of plantation songs, with many spiritual songs, such as "Wade in the Water" and "Steal Away to Jesus," serving the dual purpose of inspiration and upliftment and providing directions for escape.

In many instances, cultural and artistic expressions of the African Americans became forms of resistance and declaration of the humanity and beauty of African people. Inspiring significant cultural moments such as the "New Negro Era" or the "Negro Renaissance" that prompted migration from rural South to the Northern industrial states. There was a call for Black artists to use their talents to inspire the community to resist oppression, whereby "one stream of black aesthetic artists created works that were inspired by the revolutionary idealism of African Liberation struggles against European colonialism" (Jackson et al. of Black America, vol. V, 1095).

While some artists became a source of inspiration for political movements, others focused on cultural reclamation, whereby they created Art that celebrated traditional African culture, reflecting daily life and honoring African Kings and Queens. Many began traveling to the continent, allowing them to capture the true essence of life on the continent, and were able to learn about African Art and culture through firsthand experience.

According to the journal *Reference Library of Black America, vol. 3*, "Black families have been crafted in the context of the remembered cultures of Africa. Family life was central to African cultures and social organization, and enslaved Africans brought this value with them to America" (595).

The American value system prioritized the "nuclear family" as the ideal family structure of mother, father, and children within the same household. However, the African American family structure tends to be more blended and extended, including not only the husband and wife but also aunts, uncles, grandparents, cousins, nieces, and nephews, who may share the household for undetermined periods of time. There are also instances of recognized 'kin' who may not be blood relatives but are acknowledged and treated as being part of the family.

This extensive family structure is a continuation of a structure that stems from an African cultural value system where a support system extends to the larger community. Part of the extended family is oftentimes the grandparents, who are respected members of the community and are known to play a valuable role in assisting with raising younger generations and passing on family traditions. Recognized as the elder of the family or community, this person is afforded a level of respect and love such that it was uncommon to consider placing an elder in a care home. It was understood that it was the responsibility of family members and the larger community to ensure that the family elder's needs were taken care of.

Along with family structure, there are other cultural practices that are grounded in the African heritage. These examples can be found in common dishes, religious practices, and hairstyles. The practice of African Spirituality can be considered as an area where one can locate deeper expressions of African traditions. Due to the social construct of slavery, where Africans were forced to hide evidence of any form of cultural practices, enslaved Africans in the United States, Latin America, and the Caribbean found ways to syncretize traditional practices with other Religions, including Christianity. These newly created Spiritual traditions included herbal healing, ancestor veneration, and the use of charms and amulets for protection. Widely practiced traditions include Lucumi, Hoodoo, and Voodoo.

While spirituality plays a significant role in maintaining a connection to the continent, food and its role in maintaining sustenance and family togetherness are arguably vital cultural elements retained by enslaved Africans. During the transport to the Americans, enslaved Africans brought with them seeds, grains and knowledge that helped create a culinary culture that has left an imprint as part of America's Food culture. Some of the foods brought with the Africans include Okra, Watermelon, Coffee, Black Eye Peas, Yams, and Rice. In addition to these foods, African American inspiration to the culinary makeup of added flavors, spices, and preparation styles that are unique to other cultural groups. Some dishes, such as gumbo and jambalaya rice, have origins in Senegal, Nigeria, Benin, and Guinea.

MATUNDA YA KWANZAA (FIRST FRUITS)

Kwanzaa is a cultural holiday that begins on December 26th and ends on January 1st. It was created in 1966 by Dr. Maulana Karenga, a professor of Africana Studies, to be an African and pan-African holiday that celebrates family, community, and culture. Kwanzaa is a Swahili word meaning First Fruits. It is organized around the Nguzo Saba (The Seven Principles): Umoja (Unity), Kujichagulia (Self-Determination), Ujima (Collective Work and Responsibility), Ujama (Co-operative Economics), Nia (Purpose), Kuumba (Creativity), and Imani (Faith). These 7 principles are based on values that are meant to guide its practitioners on being the best expressions of themselves and living a life that elevates and empowers the collective.

While this holiday was not created on the continent, I strongly believe that the practice of this holiday should be adopted by those of us who see ourselves as living a lifestyle that is reflective of our Africentric identity. Kwanzaa is not just a cultural holiday that is celebrated for 7 days. It serves as a guide and reminder of how the collective should live in a way that ensures progression and "speaks to the best of what it means to be African and human in its fullest self" (officialkwanzaawebsite.org). It is a cultural expression that speaks directly to those of us who have been stripped of our heritage and fills the need for a holiday that reinforces our African cultural heritage.

Through this holiday celebration, we are given space to celebrate and embrace being African in the diaspora, which generates a sense of pride and belonging. For me, it also creates opportunities to express my African identity beyond the seven days, as Kwanzaa is meant to be a lifestyle rather than a weeklong series of activities. It has the ability to be the gateway activity for developing a true Africentric mindset and lifestyle.

Although Kwanzaa has been recognized since the 60s, there is still much work to be done to educate our community about the meaning and benefits of the practice. There are a few myths and misconceptions that I will respond to with the hopes that it will inspire some to adopt the tradition.

1. Kwanzaa is a Religion

Kwanzaa is NOT a religion in any form nor associated with any specific faith or belief system. It is strictly a blend of African and African American cultural practices that includes a list of principles meant to instruct its participants on things to embody that will serve as the foundation for the building and elevation of the community. Its practitioners do not worship or celebrate any particular being or entity but spend the seven days meditating on ways each individual can contribute to the growth of the community through economics, unity, creativity, hard work, and faith.

2. Kwanzaa is a Man-Made holiday

There is much hesitancy toward recognizing Kwanzaa as a credible holiday due to the sentiment that it is a man-made/invented holiday. We have accepted current practices and holidays as normal to the degree that a relatively new celebration that was created by someone who is still alive seems to lose validity. The point needs to be made that all holidays were, at one point, someone's idea as a means to recognize a special day or practice. Many holidays have evolved over the years to become what could be described as capitalistic tools for the promotion of spending. Kwanzaa, a cultural holiday created to honor culture, deserves the same respect despite being created within our lifetime.

3. **Kwanzaa is an African Holiday**

   Kwanzaa is a way of life. In its essence, it is meant to remind us of how we are expected to interact with each other and provide guidance for us to live in a way that elevates and empowers us with knowledge and spiritual and material wealth. It was created by an African American scholar who used the Swahili Language to describe essential elements of the holiday. However, it is not African in its origination but can be practiced by anyone of African descent. It serves to help those of us from the diaspora connect in ways other holidays or religious practices do not help us.

4. **Kwanzaa takes the place of Christmas**

   Kwanzaa starts December 26th and ends January 1st. Although it falls at the end of the holiday season, it is not meant to replace Christmas as it is neither religious nor can it be substituted for Christmas. Practicing and understanding Kwanzaa has forced me to see the wisdom in having the practice at the end of the year. It is the perfect time for those of us making New Year resolutions and setting goals to also spend time thinking about the principles and how to best live by them during the coming year. Although there are families who only recognize the cultural celebration, families can celebrate both Christmas and Kwanzaa.

ESTABLISHING MEANINGFUL CONNECTIONS

African immigrant communities can be found in most large cities across the Diaspora. Their presence also means that one can find restaurants, small shops, grocery stores, and culturally based festivals, shows, and celebrations that are open to the public. Once aware of the presence of these cultural groups, taking the bold step to participate in their activities is an ideal way to learn more about the various cultures in your city.

African immigration to the United States began with the passage of the Immigration and Nationality Act of 1965. Prior to the passage of the immigration legislation, citizenship was reserved for immigrants, mainly from Western European nations. Like most immigrant populations, newly arrived African immigrants established large communities in Urban Metropolitan cities such as New York City, Washington D.C, Florida, and Atlanta. "Approximately 2.1 million

African immigrants have resettled in the U.S. since the initial wave of immigrants in the 1970s" (blackpast.org). By 2017, roughly 4.3 million Africans and their immediate descendants resided in the U.S., with the numbers steadily increasing.

First and second-generation immigrants raised in the United States seek to maintain a cultural connection to their homeland, resulting in the popularization of modern African fashion, Afrobeats, and a curiosity about African food. Along with fashion, food, and music, cultural events and activities play an instrumental role in the continuation of cultural heritage. I must state that, depending on the city in which one lives, there may be no shortage of cultural events throughout the year. African Americans or Caribbean nationals who are fortunate to have friends from various parts of the African continent or friends who are promoters of African events will find it easy to access a variety of exciting cultures and cultural events.

Having genuine relationships with different communities helps with reaffirming one's African identity as you are able to identify similarities and find connections to your own. It also serves to fill a void a person may feel, depending on their upbringing and the extent to which there is self-awareness. Social interactions are absolutely necessary to dismantle untruths, stereotypes, and distrust that exist among newly arrived African Immigrants, African Americans, and Caribbean nationals.

For generations, there have been seeds of mistrust and misunderstanding between the groups that were intentionally sewn by European colonizers. Misinformation was fed through movies, documentaries, and cultural content that told stories that misrepresented the realities of each group while creating stereotypes and caricatures. These distorted images of each other led to building envy and distrust, which prevented or delayed the process of connecting and truly understanding each other. However, this is changing as African Americans are seeking their cultural heritage in various ways and, most importantly, taking trips to the continent, with some even moving there permanently.

Not all of us are able to or are ready to make that flight to the continent. However, there are alternative ways to establish relationships and learn about the vast array of cultural expressions. I encourage everyone to take the step to seek out local Afrobeats or Amapiano events, establish a relationship with someone from the continent, and engage in healthy conversations that allow for the exchange of information. If we can celebrate St. Patrick's Day, Cinco De Mayo, and Caribbean Carnivals in any major city, then we can be intentional about attending any African cultural event in your city.

CHAPTER 4
West Indian & Afro-Latino Culture

Nyame Dua
(God's presence and protection)

CHAPTER 4
WEST INDIAN & AFRO-LATINO CULTURE

Afro-Caribbean and Afro-Latino cultures are subcultures of the Caribbean and Latin American regions. These subcultures are distinct and unique due to the strong influences of music, food, language, and cultural practices from the African continent. Enslaved Africans in Latin America and the Caribbean have had a significant influence on the indigenous music of the region through drumming, rhythms, and call and response. The degree to which African music underpins Latin American styles such as cumbia, samba, bachata, and reggaeton highlights the need for greater acknowledgment and recognition of its origins and the people.

Other popular cultural forms with African origins or created by Afro-Latino communities would be the Rumba, Conga dance, and Mambo from Cuba and the Bomba and Plena from Puerto Rico. The Bomba was developed in the 15th and 16th Centuries by enslaved Africans as a form of music and a way to share secret messages. Certain movements told a story and sent messages that became acts of resistance. In his book *The Black Revolution on the Screen*, Horace Campbell states that "it was a source of political and spiritual expression, and the lyrics conveyed a sense of anger and sadness about their condition, and songs served as a catalyst for rebellions and uprisings" (45). When the colonizers eventually understood the underlying meaning of the dance and messages hidden in the sounds-initiated acts from the state to suppress the art form and any signs of resistance.

"Plena developed from bomba music around the beginning of the 20th century in southern Puerto Rico. Plena lyrics are narrative. They convey a story about events, address topical themes, often comment on political protest movements, and offer satirical commentaries" (folkways.si.edu). This can be compared to Calypso of Trinidad and Tobago, Reggae music of Jamaica, and Hip Hop in its early days. Africans of the Diaspora were able to use music to speak to their living conditions and their ability to survive and overcome life's challenges.

One can also find a strong African presence in spiritual and religious practices across the Americas. In an effort to practice spiritual practices with origins from the continent, enslaved Africans found ways to hide them by merging their beliefs and symbols with those of Christianity. Some religious practices include Obeah, Candomblé, Santeria, and Vodou, all common to Latin America, while Lukumi and Ifa are popular within the United States.

As for foods, Latin America and the Caribbean regions are replete with dishes originating from the African continent. Enslaved Africans introduced yams, sweet potatoes, callaloo, fish cakes, plantains, bananas, corn meal, and okra, among others. Their meals primarily consisted of ingredients that the Slave masters did not want or would only allow enslaved to eat. However, the merging of cultures with the Indigenous Indians and East Indians and the arrival of foods brought by the Europeans led to a fusion of delicacies that are unique to the region.

Some of the more popular dishes from Latin America include Tamale, Mangu, Conkie, Okro Soup, Mogo mogo, Ackee, Rice and Peas, and Mofongo, among others. I am making mention of these African-inspired practices to highlight elements of African-inspired culture that have been retained over the centuries. While the practices have evolved in the face of restrictions, they were instrumental in ensuring the continuation of spirituality to aid in the survival and empowerment of Africans in the diaspora.

Now that we have explored the concept of culture and the various forms created within the Diaspora, how do we, with intention, re-engage with an African culture for the purpose of strengthening our ties to the continent and remembering those parts that we have not been able to retain over the years?

The argument made by groups who say that they are not "African," even though there is a clear phenotypical connection, is that Africa is a large continent with hundreds of languages and ethnic groups, and it is impossible to identify a specific culture to adopt. While this may be true, the continent has a distinctly unique culture that sets it apart from other cultural groups. "We came from a culture of tremendous order, which provided us with a viable belief system, with guided behavior and moral interrelationship" (Ani 13). This includes:

- Hairstyles
- Creativity in the arts (music, art and dance)
- Sharing life with community and friends
- Fashion styles with the inclusion of bright colors
- Importance of the Family system

In studying the list above, we will recognize that what has been established as African American, Afro-Latino, and West Indian cultures are similar. The cultural impact made by the African diaspora has been significant regionally and globally, with undeniable connections to the continent. It shows the spirit of our ancestors, and Africa continues to move within us despite the continuous attempt to disconnect us from our ancestral heritage and identity.

Reestablishing ties to the continent is important and is becoming increasingly necessary because a people that is not rooted in culture is lost. A void leads to a group of people being easily swayed or influenced by values that are alien to the community.

I will, therefore, endeavor to list steps that can be taken to reestablish a connection that facilitates alignment to an African Identity. This is essential because knowing one's culture is foundational, as it:

- Supports knowledge of self
- Serves as a guide/forms habits and expectations
- Binds people together
- Is a source of pride and belonging
- And most importantly, it shows our resistance as a people

Practitioners seek to restore the spiritual practices of ancient Kemet, which included honoring the ancestors, connecting with Gods and Goddesses through rituals and prayers, and cultivating Ma'at and the cosmic order. Community is an incremental aspect of Kemeticism, as it fosters connections with like-minded people and reinforces social and cultural values. A robust Kemetic community has established Temples globally, which creates spaces for practitioners to commune in person and virtually.

STEPS TO LIVING AN
AFRICAN-CENTERED LIFESTYLE

In understanding the realities of our condition and what we have evolved to become, it is clear that we are influenced by foreign forces that are not meant to serve our best interests. We must make a decision to either maintain the status quo or take action steps to further dismantle the destructive elements of Western culture and consciously assume the identity of what it means to be African as a collective. There are and have always been segments of our community that live a life within that consciousness.

An example would be The Rastafarian movement popularized by Bob Marley. This movement is a cultural community and spiritual belief system that mixes the Bible with some African beliefs and traditions. It has its roots in the philosophy of Pan-Africanism and Political Activist Marcus Garvey, who urged the Black Diaspora to return to Africa where a Black King would be crowned. Ethiopia is identified as the Promised Land, and Haile Selassie is considered the Black messiah. Rastafarians do not believe in cutting or combing their hair, as referenced in Leviticus 19:27 of the Bible: "Do not cut the hair at the sides of your head or clip off the edges of your beard." This concept of the virtue of long locks is reiterated several times in the Bible and is a sacred belief for many African cultures.

This group was able to create a lifestyle that elevated an African-centered mindset by removing the Western Eurocentric interpretation of the Bible, thus creating a new movement, removing themselves physically, spiritually, and mentally from a world that was created to oppress and subjugate the African family. They live by the principles of a balanced natural lifestyle, eating a plant-based diet and dressing in the colors red, black, green, and gold. The colors red, black, green, and gold represent the following: red symbolizes the blood of the martyrs, black represents the people of Africa, green stands for nature and the land, and gold signifies the mineral wealth of Ethiopia.

KEMETIC SPIRITUALITY

The practice of Kemetic Spirituality is an ancient Egyptian religion that has a growing number of practitioners across the globe. Ancient Egypt is known by the name Kemet and is the place where "Kemetic Spirituality began, dating back to pre-dynastic Egypt, over 5,000 years ago" ("What is Kemetic Spirituality?"). It is "an African Traditional Religion and bears similarity to other African Traditional and African Diasporic religions, as well as spiritual practices from Northeastern Africa and the Ancient Near East" ("Kemetic Orthodoxy FAQs"). Additionally, many texts and scholars have expressed the connection between Christianity and Judaism as having been influenced by the traditions and practices of Kemeticism.

In the following chapters, I will discuss a list of ways Diasporan Africans can regain the ways and identity of our ancestors in a way that empowers and elevates the collective.

CHAPTER 5
Natural Hair

Duafe
(Femininity, nurturing, cleanliness)

CHAPTER 5
Natural Hair

DEFINITION OF A NATURAL HAIRSTYLE

Having a natural hairstyle means not manipulating the hair's natural structure as it grows out of the head in any way that changes its structure. This includes any style that does not involve perming, blowouts, or straightening of any kind. With increasing contact with European and other non-African cultures, the standard of beauty shifted to the point where straightening hair and styling forms that are unique to other cultures have become normalized to Africans.

To be considered civilized, well-groomed, professional, and attractive, African men were forced to keep their hair cut low. The acceptable professional look for women was getting a perm or straightener or wearing wigs that did not truly reflect their natural look.

In the 1960s, during the Black Power movement, there was a shift in the acceptance of Black beauty and pride in being African. Black women fought to be accepted with their natural hair in public spaces, which led to the passage of the Crown Act in 2021, which "prohibits discrimination based on a person's hair texture or hairstyle if that style or texture is commonly associated with a particular race or national origin" (congress.gov).

Popular culture of the 1970s, 80s, and 90s reintroduced fashionable styles that reversed the advancement in wearing natural hair. However, we saw a resurgence in the 2000s. Black women stopped perming and straightening their hair and started creating products that were unique to the community and specific to the range of hair textures found among Black women.

Today, popular culture is pushing an aesthetic that is normalizing an unnatural straight look for Black women. Companies and the larger society no longer need to place overt restrictions on Black women. Instead, the common look worn by celebrities, artists, and public figures encourages fake hair and lashes that are not representative of an African woman.

Many argue that there is evidence of women wearing wigs among some ethnic groups from the continent. This is true; there are images of Egyptian women wearing stylish hair coverings. The difference, however, is that those wigs were not long straight hair from an animal or from the head of an ethnic group, which is phenotypically different from the African woman.

WHY IS HAIR IMPORTANT?

The Black/African woman takes great pride in her hair. A woman's hair represents her crown, a manifestation of the love she has for herself, a choice in how she chooses to present herself to the world.

Historically, hair had significant meaning for women of a particular ethnic group. As early as the 15th century, different tribes used hair to show one's social hierarchy. Members of royalty wore elaborate hairstyles as a symbol of their stature.

"Hair was also a symbol of fertility. If a person's hair was thick, long, and neat, it symbolized that one was able to bear healthy children. If someone were in mourning, they would pay very little attention to their hair" (Matshego).

In some cultures, including the Yoruba culture, hair holds spiritual significance and is considered to have a divine connection to God due to its location on the body. Many Rastafarians also believe that their hair is their strength and weakness if cut off. They grow their hair into dreadlocks as part of the Nazarite vow, which is part of the Bible in Leviticus 21:5.

In a colonized Euro-centered world, the way we wear our natural hair became a symbol of resistance, pride, and celebration. A political statement that subtly and overtly sends a message of defiance. This spirit of resistance and defiance comes on the heels of a pattern of laws and systemic alienation as a means to control and deter the way Black men and women wear their hair.

THE USE OF LEGISLATION
TO CONTROL BLACK HAIR

Europeans understood the importance of hair in the African culture, and one of the first things the slave traders did to the people they captured was shave off their hair. "Considering the strong spiritual and cultural importance of hair in Africa, it was a particularly dehumanizing act, intended to strip away their connection to their cultures" (Odelebeauty.com).

In the 1700s, a population of Free Blacks in Louisiana County was controlled by the Spanish. This Free Black community held a unique position within colonial society in that they were "not under the control of the laws governing slavery, but they were also denied all the rights and privileges that came with being white" (noirnola.com). There was fear that they would become too powerful, and the women, due to their beauty, were attracting the attention of white men. The Louisiana Governor, in his attempt to reposition the community closer to the enslaved community, tried to control Free Black women "who had become too light-skinned or who competed too freely with white women for status, therefore threatening the social order," passed the Tignon Law.

The Tignon Law ordered Free Black women to tie their hair in a headscarf to control their excessive dressing style and the attention they were receiving. This order saw Black women taking the opportunity, like they always did, to use something that was meant to control or oppress as a means to further their creativity, strength, and intelligence. The ladies wrapped their hair in "tignons with bright, beautiful colors, jewelry, and feathers." What was meant to suppress them ended up making them even more beautiful in appearance. It was so beautiful that the European women of the colony couldn't let us have nothing,' not even the very things meant to oppress us, and began to copy and wear tignons as well" (noirnola.com).

It is imperative for us as a community to recognize that our hair type/texture is uniquely different from every other ethnic/cultural group for a reason. God, the Divine creator, was not mistaken when he chose to give us the unique hair textures that we have. It is incumbent on us to recognize that there is something special about the way our hair grows out of our head, and putting chemicals, burning, straightening, and covering with wigs (from other humans and animals) removes us further away from what it is that makes us different as a people.

CHAPTER 6
A Bold Statement of Identity & Pride

Nsaa
(Excellence, authenticity)

CHAPTER 6
A Bold Statement of Identity & Pride

Having a unique style of dress is seen as a way of self-expression. A statement that can be made boldly or subtly to show the world a part of your identity. A person's choice of fashion indicates:

- Socio-Economic Status
- Cultural affiliation
- Professional Position
- Self-Love and Self Pride

AFRICAN FASHION/STYLE

Making an intentional decision to dress daily in Africentric clothing is a bold statement demonstrating pride in one's identification with African culture. It further relays the message that the individual has an understanding of who they are culturally, which tends to draw a unique type of reaction from people in their immediate environment.

It is exciting to see a resurgence of interest in African fashion that goes beyond the Dashiki, a style of dress that was popular in the 1960s during the Black Power Movement. Diasporans have embraced the bold patterns and colorful fabrics unique to the culture and are increasingly including them in their wardrobe.

This resurgence is exciting and necessary as it shows that we are becoming comfortable with boldly expressing pride in being African. It is also exciting to see the growing number of African fashion shows organized in almost every state across the United States and in most major cities around the world, including in the Caribbean, South/Latin America, and Europe.

Increased interest in Africentric fashion has led to a surge in interest in learning about fabrics, their origins, and the meanings of their patterns. Though many of these fabrics are not made on the continent, they are still described as African, as they are made primarily for the African demographic. This means the manufactured patterns and colors are created to reflect African motifs that are sometimes unique to specific cultures. The fact that the Ankara or Kitenge fabrics are not unique to any particular grouping is critical, as it helps to make the fashion acceptable to Diasporans who are seeking to embrace their cultural heritage without feeling as though they might be co-opting a style that is meant for a specific ethnic group.

African Style and Fashion can be placed into two categories: Modern Wear and Traditional Wear. Traditional fashion includes fabrics and styles that are affiliated with a specific ethnic group on the continent and worn for special occasions such as weddings, funerals, and naming ceremonies. Some items may be intended to be worn by specific community members or individuals of a particular social ranking within the culture. Along with the particular style, the fabrics used are often unique to that culture in that they are handmade or handwoven in colors, patterns, and textures that are unique to that culture for several generations.

Modern African Fashions are clothing created using African fabric such as the Ankara or more culturally specific fabrics made on the continent. These fabrics are made into styles that are more Western in flair and cut and can be worn by anyone across cultural lines. Also, the growth of Africentric fashion has a significant economic impact. The majority of the fashion is designed and produced by local tailors, seamstresses, and designers on the continent and in the diaspora. Choosing to spend money on culturally based clothing helps to support talented designers and tailors and the growth of an emerging fashion industry.

We must acknowledge the growing presence of Chinese manufacturing of African fabrics, which continues to have a negative economic effect on the young, emerging industry. African designers, smaller tailors, and seamstresses are forced to compete with Chinese manufacturers and clothing brands, creating fast fashion with prices significantly cheaper than authentic African pieces. Customers should also be careful where they purchase their clothing, as many websites offer lower-quality products that are not made to fit properly.

It is known that the Black/African community spends millions of dollars on clothing and beauty products annually. It is part of our identity to place importance on presentation and being fashionable. If we are going to spend our dollars on these expenses, then that money should be redirected to the communities that align with our cultural identity. Along with the cultural and economic impact of wearing Africentric clothing, there is an immediate response that a person receives when they enter a space wearing a beautifully created Africentric outfit. The wearer often emanates an aura that elicits admiration and respect from those around them.

I have noticed that when Black women wear beautifully coiffed natural hairstyles while wearing African-inspired outfits that complement their style and body type, respect is elicited from observers across genders. There seems to be an immediate assumption of the lady's quality and the mindset she has about herself and her culture. Black men are most certainly not excluded. In my experience, Black/African men who dress in Africentric attire have a mindset that is rooted in community and culture. Depending on the exquisiteness of the attire, the energy felt could be that of an African King and royalty.

Apart from the external responses, internally, there is an undeniably regal feeling and pride in oneself due to the way one chooses to show up in public. Transitioning to African Fashion is both a spiritual and gradual process for those of us who did not grow up in an environment that celebrates being African. Over the years, I have come to realize that there are phases to embracing the culture. A person's sense of identity determines how "African" they are willing to present themselves.

STYLES

Dear Ladies, a culturally-rooted look does not have to be excessive. A simple pair of wooden earrings, cowrie shell accessories, or an Africa-shaped pendant is enough to send a statement that you acknowledge who you are. Any of the above items paired with bracelets, matching purses, and/or headwraps make a bold statement without saying much. The next level is an African print skirt or shorts with a solid top, headwrap, and culturally inspired accessories. These are just a few examples of simple looks that can be styled for ladies who are learning about or becoming comfortable with this new form of self-expression.

Men, on the other hand, can wear shirts with primarily solid colors accented with African print on strategic parts of the shirt, with pants that match the solid color of the shirt. The pants can also be in full

African print, similar to the accents on the shirt. A gentleman who is completely comfortable embracing fashion can wear a full African print shirt, solid pants, and culturally inspired bracelets to complement.

There is no occasion where one cannot find a reason to wear Africentric attire. It is encouraged that as we go through the process of self-acceptance and appreciation of the culture, wearing cultural attire that suits the occasion becomes the norm rather than the exception. It is time that we stand out with pride and make a defiant statement against a society that is designed to dissuade us from reflecting on our true selves.

DECORATING THE HOME AND WORKSPACE

This topic is meant to highlight the normalization of the Eurocentric lifestyle in every facet of our lives. The home is a place where we spend the most time with our families and closest friends. This is the primary space where we create bonds, establish our worldviews, and learn lessons about life, which determine how we show up in the world. Along with being a place where families build and grow, it is a form of incubator that shapes the family's quality of life and life interests. These descriptors/qualities are reflected in the items within the home that help to reinforce the family's value system. One such element, is how the house is decorated. Most of us enjoy visiting a house for the first time and noting how it is furnished and decorated or observing if there is a lack of either. We are impressed by a beautifully decorated space and can agree that the personalities of the residents are often reflected in the way the house is decorated. Therefore, like every other aspect of our lives, the place we spend the most time should be decorated and have the aesthetic to remind us of who we are culturally.

It has become common to see many homes in Arizona, for example, with the familiar items from Target, IKEA, or Ross. There is a consistent look and feel to the spaces that lack cultural personality, which fails to reaffirm the family's cultural identity. There is a significant number of artists within our community who create beautiful paintings, wall hangings, sculptures, and other decorative items for the home. However, the low level of support for these artistic talents is evident in the lack of Black art that is generally found in Black homes. There needs to be a conscious effort to purchase art and decor that reflects Black/African culture. This is important as it teaches children from a young age about cultural pride, reaffirms identity, and normalizes the act of decorating personal spaces with art that reflects our cultural identity.

CHAPTER 7
Unity & Empowerment

Bese Saka

(Affluence, power, abundance)

CHAPTER 7
Unity & Empowerment

Due to the United States being a country of immigrants, it has become commonplace to find concentrated geographical areas dedicated to specific cultural or ethnic groups. Like the popular Chinatowns, one can find central districts and enterprises created to provide for the needs of various ethnic communities. Such businesses have thrived and have become sources of diversity for many cities, exposing others to the uniqueness of their culture and contributing to the economic empowerment of the community.

SUPPORT BLACK BUSINESSES

As we seek to practice the principles of Umoja and Ujimaa (Kwanza principles of Unity and Co-operative Economics) throughout the year, I will encourage us to include African restaurants, grocery stores, clothing stores, seamstresses and tailors, and hair stylists on the list of Black/African businesses to support with intention.

We can only elevate as a people if we move in unity; therefore, supporting African businesses along with African American and Caribbean businesses should be a priority. It provides an opportunity for members of each Cultural background to become familiar with members of groups, meet new people, and help circulate the dollars within our communities. Supporting African businesses also helps to establish ties between African Americans and newly arrived Africans and helps to delegitimize the false belief that there is always distrust between the two groups.

It is understood that the attitude of distrust has been embedded into our psyche over a period of time, which has contributed to our inability to circulate our dollars within our communities. This is compounded by the fact that integration, which was meant to create a balance in access to resources, instead led to the breakdown of the community. Understandably, there were contributing factors that influenced the families to leave Black, primarily urban neighborhoods for predominantly white suburbs. This migration reinforced the perception that proximity to whiteness is better with regard to the quality of lifestyle and what we choose to spend our dollars on. There has been a reawakening of the need to support Black businesses, with many African Americans choosing to only support Black-owned businesses as much as they can. However, this decision is revolutionary as it takes intention and deliberate effort.

Various entities and individuals have created several initiatives to promote and support black-owned businesses. Such initiatives include National

Black Business Month, held in August. It is an opportunity for consumers to support Black businesses and to drive policy meant to empower Black business owners. Federally Funded Grants and programs support Black and Women-owned businesses, and a growing number of successful entrepreneurs are sharing their knowledge and expertise on social media to help educate, empower, and inspire.

Going hand in hand with circulating our dollars within our community is understanding our collective buying power and using it to enforce change. Although we do not have the political willpower similar to actions taken during the Black Power and Civil Rights era, there have been moments where attempts have been made to intentionally withhold our dollars in protest. One of the most prominent initiatives was Blackout Day, which became a day of economic protest held on July 7th, 2020. It was a day when Black shoppers were called to withhold their money from the economy, and if they were to spend money, they should only spend at Black-owned businesses.

READ BOOKS BY AFRICAN AUTHORS

Several books written by African authors speak to African culture pre-colonization and share the impact colonization has had on their societies. This is important because it gives insight into what life was like in Africa.

We all know that we have been misinformed (intentionally misled/lied to) about Africa and its history. Apart from studying African History in College/University (where information is often limited) or visiting the continent, it would benefit us diasporans to read books that are authored by Africans.

This serves to:

- Provide a perspective of life in Africa that is unfamiliar
- Eliminate misinformation and possible stereotyping
- Develop appreciation through the identification of similarities in culture
- Build empathy through the recognition of lived experiences that may be similar

Some of my favorite authors are:

- Chinua Achebe
- Malidoma Some
- Chimamanda Ngozi Adichie
- Magogodi oaMphela Makhene
- Dambisa Moyo
- Walter Rodney

SOCIAL MEDIA CHANNELS
AND INFLUENCERS TO FOLLOW

It is undeniable that we are in an information age, a time where it has become much easier to access information on almost any topic. Thanks to the internet and technology, there is a growing number of social media platforms that provide content that informs audiences about current news from the continent, share detailed analyses of developments, and present informative documentaries of historical events. These sites provide a wealth of information that is not available through traditional media. For years, we complained that we lacked knowledge of self due to information being hidden from us and not being taught our full history in the school system. However, over time, it has become significantly easier to access information relating to African history and culture.

There are Pan-African thought leaders who have established platforms specializing in topics ranging from politics to culture to spirituality. I see them as the teachers we may not have had in school and an opportunity to gain knowledge of self, outside of a structured classroom or conference room setting.

Along with listening to current thought leaders, it is imperative that we study the teachings and speeches of past leaders who spent their lives fighting for the progression of the global African people. We grew up with knowledge of key historical figures such as

George Washington, Abraham Lincoln, and Christopher Columbus; however, we do not have enough knowledge about Marcus Garvey, Kwame Nkrumah, and John Henrik Clark.

It is time that we are intentional about the content we consume. Given the access our cell phones, laptops, or television have given us, they must be seen as tools to empower, inform, and inspire and not only as a means of distraction and entertainment. Along with learning about the teachings of key historical figures, it is also important to follow the social media platforms that are dedicated to specific cultural or national groups. I have gained intimate knowledge of aspects of different cultures as a result of the information shared.

CHAPTER 8
Ancestral Discovery &
African Reconnection

Nea Onnim
(Pursuit of knowledge)

CHAPTER 8
Ancestral Discovery & African Reconnection

Considered one of the more controversial steps towards knowledge of self and cultural awareness, taking a DNA test to determine one's ancestry is the ideal way to trace one's ancestral lineage and rediscover self. While there has been hesitancy to share one's DNA with companies, there is yet to be evidence of misuse of data or DNA samples provided to companies. I would argue that having the ability to trace ancestral lineage and place of origin prior to the kidnapping and enslavement of Africans is revolutionary. It helps us decide which cultural events to attend, which books to read, and which specific ethnic group to study in our quest for the origins of our ancestors.

DISCOVER AFRICAN ANCESTRY
THROUGH DNA TESTING

Dr. Henry Louis Gates Jr. can be considered as being instrumental in popularizing the discovery of ancestral lineage using DNA testing. His show 'Finding Your Roots' featured influential Americans who were provided information about their ancestry through scientific methods, which oftentimes provided unexpected details about their family history. While

Dr. Gates worked with geneticists and genealogists connected to academic institutions he was affiliated with, companies that provide similar services to interested persons have since been established. The company that seems to be the most concise with the information provided would be *African Ancestry*. It serves as an important additional form of self-discovery and re-connection to ancestral lineage.

There are numerous stories of people benefiting from learning about their lineage to the point where they are inspired to travel to their ancestral homeland to gain a deeper knowledge of self apart from traveling. One can find communities on social media networks created to help individuals establish connections with other diasporans on similar journeys, identify culturally specific events to attend, and seek out businesses and community centers. These are all intentional actions we can take to help us on our journey of reconnection.

TRAVEL TO CITIES AND COUNTRIES

In 2019, the Ghanaian government, working in collaboration with a group of notable African Americans, established an initiative that led to thousands of Diasporan Africans visiting the continent to celebrate, honor, learn, and reconnect to their ancestry. This series of events culminated in "The Year of Return," a significant spiritual and birthright journey inviting the global African family, both at home and abroad, to mark the 400th anniversary of the arrival of the first enslaved Africans in Jamestown, Virginia. This event is arguably the most significant initiative to reconnect the continent with its diasporans, helping to forge ties that helped to heal wounds and build bridges between worlds and peoples who were forcibly separated.

This event, however, is not the first of its kind to draw diasporans to the continent. Between 1800 and 1890, the Back-To-Africa Movement mobilized thousands of Black Americans to return to their ancestral homeland. The desire to return peaked and waned over the years, depending on social conditions across the diaspora. The Caribbean, in particular, has contributed to a robust diasporic community across the continent as an alternative to living under colonial control. Cultural influences like reggae and the Rastafarian movement helped to serve as a reminder that Africa is our ancestral homeland and the place we should all strive to visit or migrate to.

Most notable are the Black Conscious Movement led by Marcus Garvey and the Pan-African Movement founded by Sir Henry Sylvester Williams. The spirit of both movements is kept alive today by the growing number of individuals and groups making efforts to reconnect. Evidently, there has been a shift in the perception of what it means to be African and to be connected to the continent spiritually and culturally. Each year, more diasporans are intentionally planning vacations to not only cities with large Black populations but also to the African continent. Something that was not common 10 years ago.

These are truly exciting times to be alive. There is a clear shift in the relationship between diasporans and Africa as efforts are made to re-establish connection and change negative perceptions and stereotypes. For those of us who are still unsure, research is strongly recommended, as is choosing a destination that includes learning about our brothers and sisters in the wider diaspora or on the continent.

LEARN AN AFRICAN LANGUAGE

Language is spiritual. Language is the entryway to a culture and the people of that culture. Words have power that draws its own energy; therefore, communicating in a language that speaks to the essence of who we are is important. According to Maya Angelou, "Words mean more than what is set down on paper. It takes human voice to infuse them with deeper meaning." For this reason, one cannot truly connect to the essence of being African without learning the language of our ancestors.

One of the things stripped away from us is our ability to communicate in our mother tongue. It was replaced with a foreign language that contains words that do not carry the energized connection to divinity, nature, and interaction with each other. I challenge you to select a language based on your personal interest in learning. I have committed myself to learning one diasporic language (Haitian patois) and one continental language (Swahili). Those two languages were chosen for strategic reasons.

Firstly, I consider Haiti to be the most important Black nation in the diaspora as it embodies much of everything we are and hope to be. A people with a fighting spirit founded on African pride, strength, and spirituality that cannot be defeated. Secondly, Swahili is important because it is the single most spoken African-based language on the continent. The African Union has identified Swahili as an official working language, and attempts are being made to have Kiswahili taught in schools across the continent.

It is a language originally from the coastal Swahili culture of Eastern Africa. Under the influence of Arabian traders, it became the lingua franca used by several Bantu-speaking ethnic groups. It is currently the official language of Tanzania, Kenya, Uganda, and the Democratic Republic of Congo.

For Diasporan Africans who have taken the DNA test and know their ancestry, the opportunity to learn a language associated with their ancestral heritage is a crucial element of their spiritual return. I would also be bold enough to suggest studying the Medu Ntr

(Medu Neter), the language of Ancient Kemet, which is considered one of the first written languages. It can be found engraved on the walls of pyramids and provides insight into the life and spiritual practices of our Kemetic ancestors. Individuals practicing African Spirituality may be required to learn the language of the African spiritual practice in which they are being initiated as part of the initiation process.

AFRICAN SPIRITUALITY

There are different paths to self-discovery and re-connection to ancestral lineage. However, the most powerful and impactful is being at a place where there is a spiritual rebirth of self. African people are, by nature, spiritual beings guided by our ancestors, the Creator, and spiritual guides to live the life destined for us. However, due to the circumstances of bondage and prejudice, too many of us are disconnected from having that unique spiritual relationship and practice that serves to embody our true African selves.

There is prejudice and distrust for our spiritual practices that have been in practice for thousands of years prior to the advent of Abrahamic religions. This mistrust, fear, and bias came about at the time of colonization, when we were taught to disassociate ourselves from the practices of our forefathers. Practices that held the fabric of the society together functioned as a guide for the community and played a role in the elevation and expansion of the societies. In spite of this, many of us are seeking and taking that path of spiritual discovery that is helping to elevate us and hasten the shift toward empowerment.

There are several African Spiritual practices that will lead to spiritual growth and elevation, but what is most important is acknowledging one's ancestral lineage, knowing their names, and building a relationship with them. We do this unconsciously for other cultures every time we call their names, study, celebrate, and honor the names of the people held in high esteem by the Western world. It is time for us to do the same for our heroes and heroines from the Diaspora and the African continent, especially those who are a part of our ancestral lineage.

I am of the conviction that African peoples globally will not attain true freedom until we return to our original spiritual practices. This belief is supported by the recognition that all successful revolts were a result of our spirituality being centered and calling on our ancestors for guidance. The Haitian Revolution and the successful revolts by Maroons across the Caribbean and South America are some examples. There are stories of enslaved Africans who called upon their spiritual guides and ancestors as they escaped bondage on their way to the afterlife or freedom in the Physical world.

There is power in acknowledging;
there is power in remembering.

IFA SPIRITUAL PRACTICE

In the following section, I am honored to present the valuable insights of Oloye Oladipupo Olanrewaju, an expert contributor from Odewale Land, as he shares his knowledge of the Ifa spiritual practice.

What is Ifa?

It is said that before birth and coming into the world, each person makes an agreement with the creator (Olorun/Olodumare) about the purpose of his or her life. We forget this at the time of our birth, but it remains with us as a guide (ori/head), though its voice is drowned by the roar of living in this chaotic world. The Ifa divination system helps people shape their lives in line with this deep purpose if you are struggling with some part of your life—a choice, an opportunity, illness, death, or something else and want to know how to change it for the better.

Ifa, as a Yoruba African spiritual tradition, is a complex and multifaceted system of beliefs, practices, and traditions that originated among the Yoruba people of West Africa, specifically in present-day western Nigeria, Togo, and Benin. It is a rich and dynamic tradition that encompasses various aspects of Yoruba culture, philosophy, and spirituality.

Philosophy: Ifa is a worldview that emphasizes balance, harmony, and interconnectedness.

Divination: Ifa is a system of divination that uses sacred texts (Odu Ifa) to guide individuals toward their destiny.

Spirituality: Ifa connects practitioners with the divine, ancestors, and Orisa (Yoruba deities).

Culture: Ifa is deeply rooted in Yoruba culture, reflecting its history, values, and traditions.

KEY COMPONENTS:

1. **Odu Ifa:** 256 sacred verses that contain wisdom, teachings, and guidance.
2. **Ikin Ifa:** Divination instrument (palm nuts or shells) used to access Odu Ifa.
3. **Babalawo:** Trained priest/diviner who interprets Odu Ifa.
4. **Ifa Initiation:** Ritualistic process of becoming a practitioner.

Ifa, a Yoruba African spiritual tradition, includes:

1. **Olodumare:** The supreme God, creator, and ultimate authority.
2. **Orisa:** Deities or divine beings who serve as intermediaries between Olodumare and humans.

3. **Ancestors:** Revered for guidance, wisdom, and protection.
4. **Ifa:** A system of divination that uses sacred texts (Odu Ifa) to guide individuals toward their destiny.
5. **Egungun:** Ancestor masks and masquerades that honor the ancestors.
6. **Babalawo:** Trained priests and diviners who interpret Ifa and guide individuals.
7. **Rituals and ceremonies:** Marking important life transitions and milestones and honoring Orisa and their ancestors.
8. **Spiritual growth:** Emphasis on personal development, self-discipline, and responsibility.

The Yoruba African spiritual tradition values:

1. **Community:** Collective well-being and harmony.
2. **Respect:** For elders, tradition, and the divine.
3. **Balance:** Between physical and spiritual realms.
4. **Wisdom:** Seeking guidance from Orisa, ancestors, and Ifa.
5. **Self-discovery:** Understanding one's destiny and purpose.

WHO ARE AFRICAN ANCESTORS?

It is important to understand the law of thermodynamics, which states that "energy can neither be created nor destroyed, only transformed from one form to another." With this in mind, you will realize that you are not existing for the first time; rather, you are a manifestation of the eternal energy taking on a new form in this material world.

As such, when you venerate your ancestors and remember them, you send a vibration into the eternal thread of energy that has manifested you in this time and space. Your DNA is a storage device of tens of thousands of pieces of information passed down to you from several generations past. It is a history of your many transformations from time to time. It contains both your mistakes of the past and the victories of the past.

African ancestors refer to the deceased relatives and forebears of African people, including parents, grandparents, great-grandparents, and beyond. They are believed to possess wisdom, knowledge, and spiritual power, which they use to guide and protect their living descendants.

Having the opportunity to tap into it helps you to know what to do to avoid repeated pitfalls and what to do to rise above present-day challenges. This is one scientific way to understand our African spirituality. We don't just venerate our Ancestors / Egúngún because we want to eat the meals; we do so because, in African culture, Ancestors play a vital role in the lives of their descendants, serving as a connection to the past, a guide for the present, and a bridge to the future. The reverence for ancestors is deeply ingrained in African traditions, and their legacy continues to shape the identity and values of African people.

SIGNIFICANCE OF ANCESTORS IN AFRICAN CULTURE

1. **Spiritual Guidance:** Ancestors are believed to serve as intermediaries between the living and the divine, offering guidance, protection, and wisdom.

2. **Cultural Preservation:** Ancestors are credited with passing down traditions, customs, and values that define African identity.

3. **Family Ties:** Ancestors strengthen family bonds, as descendants seek to honor and emulate their examples.

4. **Community Building:** Ancestors unite communities through shared heritage and collective memory.

WAYS OF HONORING ANCESTORS

1. **Ancestor Veneration:** Offerings, prayers, and rituals are performed to honor and appease the ancestors and seek blessings from ancestors.

2. **Storytelling:** Oral traditions preserve ancestral stories, teachings, and histories.

3. **Rituals:** Ceremonies and festivals to honor the ancestors and mark important life transitions, connecting individuals to their ancestral heritage.

4. **Ancestral Shrines:** Sacred spaces dedicated to honoring and communicating with ancestors.

In conclusion, African ancestors are revered for their wisdom, guidance, and contributions to the rich cultural heritage of the continent. By honoring ancestors, Africans connect with their past, build strong communities, and forge a brighter future. Their significance extends beyond the spiritual realm, influencing daily life, cultural traditions, and community values.

Oloye Oladipupo Olanrewaju

Borokini Awo of Odewale Land

Expert Contributor

CHAPTER 9
Rebuilding & Reinventing Community

Abusua Pa
(Good family, community values)

CHAPTER 9
REBUILDING & REINVENTING COMMUNITY

"A true community begins in the hearts of the people involved. It is not a place of distraction but a place of being. It is not a place where you reform, but a place you go home to."

"In a community, it is possible to restore a supportive presence for one another rather than distrust or competitiveness with one another. The others in the community are the reason that one feels the way one feels. The elder cannot be an elder if there is no community to make him an elder. The young boy cannot feel secure if there is no elder whose silent presence gives him hope in life. The adult cannot be who he is unless there is a strong sense of presence of the other people around. This interdependency is what I call supportive presence."

"A community is a place of self-definition. Any group of people meeting with the intention of connecting to the power within is a community."

"Without a community, you cannot be yourself. The community is where we draw the strength needed to effect changes inside of us. Community is formed each time more than one person meets for a purpose."

The "Development of a community depends on what the people involved consent to. What one acknowledges in the formation of the community is the possibility of doing together what is impossible to do alone. What we want is to create a community that meets the intrinsic needs of every individual. The individual can finally discover within the community something to relate to because deep down inside each of us is a craving for an honoring of our individualism."

The above excerpts were taken from the book *Ritual: Power, Healing and Community* written by Malidoma Some. These provide an explanation of how a community should look and feel. When we speak of community, oftentimes, it is in the context of a group of people of like mind and interest coming together for a single purpose. However, the purpose may vary depending on the interest and goals. In the context of the African (Black) culture, we need to decide as a collective, without the interference of outside forces, what community looks like for us and the role it fulfills in the 21st century.

We live in a society that is influenced by a Eurocentric framework and ideals accompanied by years of social factors that have removed people of African descent from the original construct of community. We all know the term "it takes a village to raise a child," and many of us have nostalgic memories of the time when we lived in communities where elders were respected, children were openly disciplined, and all the neighbors knew each other. However, as we gain perceived individual success and access to the Western materialistic lifestyle, the presence of a strong positive community dissipates.

The Western/Eurocentric ethos leans heavily on individualism, whereby success is determined by material gains and a superstructure where a few control the well-being of many. The family unit is removed as the source of support and replaced by a power structure or institutions that provide the needs of the individuals within a society. African people understand the value of family and community. This is evident by the actions of newly freed slaves across the diaspora who, after leaving the plantations, spent days searching for loved ones who experienced forced separation from family members during slavery. In places like the Caribbean, across Latin America, and the Southern United States, Freed Africans pooled money they earned from working to purchase land that they used to create communities. You can find these communities in every country that had an enslaved African population.

Family is the backbone of society in Africa, and it impacts every segment of the community. The concept of a child having several cousins, aunties, and Uncles who may not be blood relatives but still demand the same respect as such is intrinsically African. These family ties become part of the extended families and create opportunities for lifelong bonds and space for the provision of support for the daily routines of life, including raising a child. However, various factors, such as the Government's attack on the Black Family and a flood of drugs and weapons into our communities, have sewn distrust and dislike for our Brothers and Sisters. This is further compounded by Integration into white society during the Civil Rights Movement; individual access to materialistic individual success has given us the illusion that we are doing well economically, which stifles the desire to actively rebuild a strong community.

FORMING A COMMUNITY

How do we form a community in the 21st century? What does it look like? Before we explore what a healthy and productive community looks like, I want to look at the composition of the word community by which we can find UNITY.

Unity: The state of being united or joined as a whole.

Community: A group of people with a common characteristic or interest living together within a larger society. A feeling of fellowship with others as a result of sharing common attitudes, interests, and goals.

Understanding the definition of the word is important because it is not possible to have one without another. To have a strong, thriving community without being united in its truest form.

I attended a community forum organized by Rev. Warren Stewart Sr. that was titled "The State of Black Liberation in Arizona: Where we were then and where we are now." The conversation was heavy on bridging gaps within the community, healing from traumas, and fixing the disconnect between the Old Guard and the Younger generation. During the discussion, the question was asked, where is the Black community? The responses included: 1) one must create the kind of community that one desires, and 2) there are various types of communities in Black Arizona. Depending on your interests and city, you will find one that suits you. While this may all be true, I find such responses to be counterproductive, and they ensure that there are continued fractures and fissures within the community.

As a people, it is time that we remove distinctions that are real but also superficial so that they do not serve to prevent us from working together as a collective. It is time that we take intentional steps to be a collective that moves in unison according to agreed-upon principles, values, and goals. Therefore, the question that should be explored is what a unified community should look like. This is important because in answering this question, we know what it is that we are creating. We then understand the steps to be taken towards the direction of that vision.

What factors are needed to help create a community? Shared experiences, common interests, a shared culture and belief system, common goals, and a value system that includes love, family bonds, and an understanding that we need a community to elevate and be examples of our best selves as individuals.

Communities can be formed in spaces where like-minded individuals gather for the purposes of learning and growing together with the understanding that we are Africans who are working as a unit to achieve agreed goals. All individuals are supported by a system of practices, principles, and values that guide and direct members toward their common goal. The goals of the community are influenced by the cultural and spiritual ethos and social construct agreed on by the members as being a reflection of who they are.

Is it necessary to be in the same physical environment to be considered as having a true community? Is it possible to grow and build a community without its members living in the same physical space? In the decades following the Civil War, freed slaves and their descendants accumulated 19 million acres of land. During the Reconstruction period, Black landowners purchased every available and affordable plot of land that they could" (fairfarmsnow.org). Others acquired land that was seized from Southern landowners who did not pay taxes to the Union.

The Gullah/Geechee people of the Low Country region of the United States are an African American ethnic group originating from the rice-growing region of West Africa. This group is one of many that was successful in acquiring land, which has been passed down over the generations without lawyers and legal documentation. In Guyana, Colombia, and Suriname, one can find entire communities and villages built by African descendants of enslavement that help to retain African cultural traditions, arts, and crafts.

While there are several examples of African communities retained over the centuries, the majority of our populations live in communities and Urban spaces that do not provide communal support and have lost the quality of life that sustains African ancestral culture. Though it is possible to embark on a personal journey of self-discovery without close proximity to cultural reinforcement, it is imperative to have access to spaces that accommodate physical interaction, learning, spiritual growth, and cultural bonding.

We are at a point where it is important that, as individuals and as a collective, we find ways to establish communities among ourselves. For this endeavor to be successful and sustainable, three major elements are needed.

1. Knowledge: Knowing who we are as a people means knowing our history, understanding where we came from, and knowing the ways of our ancestors. A major reason there is a disconnect is that we are missing information, and we need to reaffirm our identity and build our spiritual essence as African people.

2. Heal Thyself: There is a need for physical and spiritual reawakening that needs to take place for all of us, particularly in the West, living in an oppressive system. There continues to be a constant attack on our minds and bodies, which affects the way we see ourselves, how we treat each other, and how we perceive our position in the world. Physical healing comes with taking care of one's body—living a healthy lifestyle that eliminates toxic elements through a healthy diet and exercise.

Spiritual healing comes in the form of Prayers, meditation, and gaining knowledge that reinforces a spiritual connection to self, community, and the universal source, the creator. As we work on healing, it is important that we find ourselves in spaces and around people that serve to reinforce the chosen path. Seek or create healthy Brotherhood and Sisterhood circles that reinforce and support that path.

3. Love for oneself and Community in its Truest Form: For African people to have been overpowered globally for several centuries, there must have been a deep level of disconnect from culture and from self—a removal of love for everything we represent and for each other as a people. It shows up every day in the way we interact and treat each other. This will not change overnight. It is time for a relearning of what love in its truest form means and what that looks like for people who have been robbed of the ability to express love for each other for centuries because we are busy trying to survive the onslaught of continuous attacks on our psyche and physical presence.

Love for oneself and for each other automatically deepens in a genuine way through self-exploration, self-discovery, and a deeper understanding of each other and the community as a whole. It creates a space for understanding and empathy, which shifts the way we interact with each other. Love also illuminates who our true enemies are, what we are fighting for and gives clarity on our collective purpose.

WHY IS COMMUNITY NECESSARY NOW?

A strong family system and community serve as a buffer from outside forces that continuously work to destabilize the Black family structure. They also serve as a support system when life gets difficult, thus preventing individuals from being dependent on a government and system that was not created to help the Black community in a sustainable way. The system reinforces identity and cultural values that serve as a guide for members of the community.

Today, we need community and a strong family unit to serve as defenses against key systems put in place that continue to weaken us. The argument can be made that the four major systems that contribute to the deterioration of our communities are the Media, the Education system, the Food System, and the Justice System. Social media and the Education Systems have replaced the family unit and larger community as a means of instructing, informing, and reinforcing culture about how we are expected to treat and interact with each other. Both systems are controlled by a power structure created to mislead and miseducate us from an early age. As a mother and teacher, I understand firsthand the impact of technology on the development of the child.

As the fabric of our community disintegrates due to our social institutions no longer playing an instrumental role in reinforcing value systems, our point of reference becomes social media and a popular culture that is generated out of media and entertainment boardrooms and not from the communities we are a part of. Social media has, in many ways, replaced the neighborhood, church, and family settings in shaping what our children understand about Black culture and Black identity. The education system is doubly damaging because the school environment should serve as an additional opportunity for a child to learn about their history and culture. Instead, the Education System has become more harmful for our Black children as it perpetuates White worldviews and knowledge that lacks cultural affirmation and pride of self.

Luckily, we live in a time when more people are becoming aware of the importance of eating healthily. We are also learning about the harmful nature of the foods that are easily accessible in our communities. According to the National Institute of Health, unhealthy nutritional intake contributes to depression and obesity. and cardiovascular diseases, among other conditions. Although many of us have nostalgic connections to particular foods we have grown up eating, it is necessary for us to make adjustments in our diet so that we can function in our ideal state and make positive contributions to the community.

The established Justice system has proven to us that it is not the ideal place for the rehabilitation of our community members who made poor decisions and found themselves caught up in the system. It would be ideal for us to create a system within our communities where we have trusted leaders who are responsible for reinforcing expectations, mediating disputes, and administering consequences as agreed by the community. Where there are structures in place to serve as preventative measures, there is less dependence on the existing legal system.

Along with a judicial structure, members of our communities face various life challenges and should find comfort in knowing that a support system exists within the community. This includes the single mother with little to no support who is overwhelmed by her responsibilities, the father who is depressed by his inability to provide, the child who feels unloved, and the elder who feels unseen and hurt.

CHAPTER 10
Bringing Authenticity to Africentricity

Sunsum (Ntoro)
(Spiritual essence, authenticity)

CHAPTER 10
Bringing Authenticity to Africentricity

"Post Traumatic Slave Diet...One of the last vestiges of
slavery can be found on our plate."
Dr. Jawanza Kunjufu

THE IMPORTANCE OF DETOXING AND DIETING

I define being authentic as the stripping away of the
things that prevent us from embodying the elements
of what it means to be purely African in our thoughts,
actions, behaviors, interactions with each other,
habits, and ethos. Being authentic is an ideal that
entails a lifestyle change, which can range from a
change of diet to detoxing. Those of us who are health
conscious and have done a detox before understand its
value. Detoxing is the process of removing impurities
from our body to aid in peak functioning. A diet of
fruits, fruit juices, and water after a short period of
fasting aids in detoxing the body. Herbs, teas, and
supplements also provide necessary nutrients while
removing toxins.

In this book, I am suggesting intentional action
steps and lifestyle adjustments meant to reduce self-
hate, low self-esteem, and lack of unity caused by years
of miseducation, brainwashing, and indoctrination
affecting Africans both on the continent and in the

diaspora. These steps will help us return to being individuals who are fully African in our essence.

A typical detox diet involves a period of fasting, followed by a strict diet of fruit, vegetables, fruit juices, and water. Sometimes, a detox also includes herbs, teas, supplements, and colon cleanses or enemas.

THE CONSEQUENCES OF NOT DETOXING OR DIETING

The passage of the Emancipation Proclamation in 1865 came at the helm of the Civil War, which lasted for 4 years and cost the lives of over 620,000 Americans. It was shrouded in controversy as the country dealt with how to best move forward on the Negro Problem—a split between the Northern and the Southern States. The former, supported by the government of the day, wanted to end slavery in support of a capitalist free market system. The latter, did not want to disrupt their economic stability and could not conceive of a world where the enslaved Africans were not under the supervision of their white "overseers."

The Emancipation Proclamation, issued on January 1, 1863, declared the freedom of enslaved Africans in the Confederate states. The Union Army, which helped secure the victory, supported it. Two years later, the Thirteenth Amendment of the Constitution was ratified, formally abolishing slavery throughout the land.

While there was widespread relief and celebration, African Americans soon learned that freedom from physical bondage did not mean the balancing of the scales of justice or an acceptance of their humanity. However, African Americans were determined to become successful contributing members of society as they worked hard to establish families and formed communities while starting businesses and institutions that supported the needs of their members. Progress, however, did not come without its fair share of disruptions, riots, and disturbances, as they made the best in an environment that consisted of disappointments, lynchings, inequality, and poverty.

While there is no denying the ability of Africans to overcome the worst of situations and survive unimaginable conditions, there is no denying that there continue to be lasting effects on the psyche of the Africans on the continent and throughout the Diaspora. This sustained condition is a result of systems of slavery and colonization, along with sustained disenfranchisement that has been institutionalized globally. There are identifiable differences and similarities in the way consistent racial oppression lasting over 600 years, starting with European first contact on the continent, has affected Global Africans.

The most pervasive and prevalent conditions that have resulted are:

- Chronic illnesses
- Low Self Esteem
- Self-Hate
- High rates of Intraracial Violence
- Multigenerational Trauma

Sadly the African descendants of enslavement have not had the space and time to deal with the trauma and burden caused by centuries of oppression. In fact, we are told to forget and dismiss our experiences. Our unacknowledged experiences have led to conditions that have manifested themselves in behaviors that have become normalized within our communities. These normalized behaviors are then accepted as being "part of the culture and just the way we are," as opposed to being recognized as manifestations of a racially oppressive system. Therefore, it can be said that while we can identify elements of our customs and traditions that derive from the continent, there are aspects of who we are that are born out of trauma and stress that need to be diagnosed and treated.

CONCLUSION

One cannot deny the impact that centuries of Colonization and being victims of enslavement have had on the psyche of the Africans on the continent and across the diaspora. The effect reveals itself in many ways, including the denial of ancestral lineage to the continent. Shame, anger, miseducation, and ignorance can all be factors in the denial of many. As the famous Bob Marley once said, there is a need to "separate ourselves from mental slavery as only we ourselves can free our minds." Frantz Fanon also explored themes related to the double consciousness of the black man, caught between two worlds and unsure how to find his way back. Although they are melanated and appear to be of African descent, there is a choice to affiliate with other cultures that are not reflective of being African.

This book is for those who are stuck between two worlds, unsure how to explore Africentric identity, and want to learn. It is also for those of us who are living the Africentric life, identify as African or Black, and seek a better knowledge of self by practicing the lifestyle described in the book, which can be considered ideal for the creation of the community that we need.

ADINKRA SYMBOLS

The symbols you see throughout this book, and on the pages to come, are **Adinkra symbols**. Adinkra symbols are visual symbols originally created by the Akan people of Ghana and the Gyaman people of Côte d'Ivoire. These symbols represent values, concepts, proverbs, and historical events, often conveying messages about unity, strength, and wisdom. Adinkra symbols are used in fabrics, pottery, logos, and architecture, and they carry profound spiritual and philosophical meanings. They serve as a form of communication and cultural expression, reflecting the beliefs, traditions, and history of the Akan and Gyaman peoples.

ADINKRA SYMBOLS

 Funtumfrafu Denkyemfrafu
(Unity in diversity)

 Wawa Aba
(Perseverance, toughness)

 Sankofa
(Learning from the past)

 Nyame Dua
(God's presence and protection)

 Duafe
(Femininity, nurturing, cleanliness)

ADINKRA SYMBOLS

Nsaa
(Excellence, authenticity)

Bese Saka
(Affluence, power, abundance)

Nea Onnim
(Pursuit of knowledge)

Abusua Pa
(Good family, community values)

Sunsum (Ntoro)
(Spiritual essence, authenticity)

ABOUT THE AUTHOR

Zoe Sarabo

Born and raised in Georgetown, Guyana, **Zoe Sarabo** migrated to Arizona to attend Arizona State University. She received her bachelor's in history and African and African American Studies. She completed her Master's in Liberal Studies program in one year with an emphasis on Borders, Migration, and Culture. Zoe credits the African and African American Studies Department and the Black and African Coalition for creating a safe environment to explore and learn about our Black Identity while lighting the spark that has become my lifelong passion.

Zoe started her career in Non-Profit work as the Economic Development Coordinator at a Community Development Corporation. She then transitioned to a Refugee Resettlement Agency, where she was tasked with providing supportive services to new immigrants. Programs ranged from Business Development support to Activities curated around culture that provided social and emotional support. During this time, she taught at ASU within the African and African American Studies Department, then transitioned to full-time teacher in 2019 at the middle school level for three years.

In 2015, Zoe organized a successful fashion show, where she received a significant number of positive reviews. Recognizing there was a need in the valley, Zoe made the decision to learn about the business and craft of African Fashion. She traveled to several cities, including Philadelphia and Los Angeles, where she attended African festivals and fashion Districts and visited local boutiques.

She was also invited and made the trip to Ghana, West Africa, where she was fortunate to connect with talented local tailors, seamstresses, and designers, visit their internationally known fabric market, and establish relationships with artisans and other creatives. During that time, she started her clothing brand and began creating pieces that were African-inspired but with a modern flair.

Her customer base quickly grew over the years alongside the growth in popularity of African style, food, and Music. She was fortunate to play a leading role in the very successful African Festival of 2019 and looks to expand the presence of African culture through the curation of the Pan African Food Festival and other programs.

While culture has been a constant area of interest, Zoe has been simultaneously developing her interest in teaching. She was fortunate to teach at both the collegiate and Middle School levels while also pursuing speaking engagements at various events in the Valley. Through life's unexpected pathway, Zoe has become a leading voice in highlighting the value and importance of connecting to the African Cultural Identity.

CONTACT INFORMATION

Email: Zoe_Sarabo@yahoo.com

REFERENCES

Adejumobi, Saheed. "The Pan-African Congress, 1900-1945." BlackPast.org, July 30, 2008, https://www.blackpast.org/global-african-history/pan-african-congresses-1900-1945/

Brooks, Christopher A. "Sacred Musical Traditions." Reference Library of Black America Vol. IV, Proteus Enterprises, 2000, p. 957.

Byrd, Ayana D., and Lori L. Tharps. Hair Story: Untangling the Roots of Black Hair in America. St. Martin's Press, 2001.

Campbell, Horace. The Black Revolution on the Screen. University of Illinois Press, 2008.

Chenier, Cierra. "The Tignon Law: How Black Women Formed Décor Out of Oppression." Noirnola.com, March 25, 2019, https://www.noirnnola.com/post/the-tignon-law-how-black-women-formed-decor-from-oppression

Du Bois, W.E.B. The Souls of Black Folk. Penguin Books, 1996.

Griffin, Chante. "How Natural Black Hair at Work Became a Civil Rights Issue." Daily.jstor.org, July 3rd, 2019, https://daily.jstor.org/how-natural-black-hair-at-work-became-a-civil-rights-issue/

Jackson, Phyllis J. "Visual and Applied Arts." Reference Library of Black America Vol. V, Proteus Enterprises, 2000, p. 1095.

"CROWN Act." H.R.5309, 116th Congress, 2020. Congress.gov, www.congress.gov/bill/116th-congress/house-bill/5309.

Kentake, Meserette. "Henry Sylvester Williams: The Father of Pan-Africanism." KentakePage.com, February 19, 2018. https://kentakepage.com/henry-sylvester-williams-the-father-of-pan-africanism/

"Kemetic Orthodoxy." Kemet.org,
https://www.kemet.org/node/584

Ngomane, Mungi. UBUNTU: Living Better Together, the African Way. HarperCollins, 2019.

Odele. "6 Things Everyone Should Know About Black Hair History." Odelebeauty.com, February 22, 2021.
https://odelebeauty.com/blogs/the-rinse/black-hair-history-facts

Osei-Kusi, Kofi. "Pan-Africanism is Spiritual." YouTube, June 2024,
https://www.youtube.com/watch?v=alC7TBAUkQ0

Patrice Some, Malidoma. Ritual: Power, Healing and Community. Penguin Books, 1993.

Richards, Akilah. Raising Free People: Unschooling as Liberation and Healing Work. PM Press, 2020.

Smithsonian. "Puerto Rican Bomba and Plena – Shared Traditions – Distinct Rhythm." Folkways.si.edu,
https://folkways.si.edu/puerto-rican-bomba-plena-shared-traditions-distinct-rhythms/latin-world/music/article/smithsonian

The Spiritual Parrot. "Kemetic Spirituality: 7 Principles of Kemetic Spirituality & Teachings." Thespiritualparrot.com, May 4th, 2022, https://thespiritualparrot.com/kemetic-spirituality/#Ancient_Kemetic_Spirituality_The_history_of_Kemetic_spirituality

"What is Culture." Palomar.edu/Anthro/culture, May 26, 2006.
https://www.palomar.edu/anthro/culture/culture_1.htm

Friends of the African Union. (n.d.). The Pan-African Congresses. Retrieved from https://friendsoftheafricanunion.com/african-diaspora/the-pan-african-congresses/

BECOMING AUTHENTICALLY AFRICAN

A GUIDE TO EMBRACING CULTURE IN EVERYDAY LIFE

Made in the USA
Columbia, SC
24 December 2024